Adventure Girls!
STEM Crafts

ADVENTURE GIRLS! STEM CRAFTS

40 Activities for
Curious, Creative, Courageous Girls

MEGAN OLIVIA HALL, PHD, MAED

ILLUSTRATED BY CAIT BRENNAN

ROCKRIDGE PRESS

For general information on our other products and services or to obtain technical support, please contact our Customer Care Department within the United States at (866) 744-2665, or outside the United States at (510) 253-0500.

Rockridge Press publishes its books in a variety of electronic and print formats. Some content that appears in print may not be available in electronic books, and vice versa.

TRADEMARKS: Rockridge Press and the Rockridge Press logo are trademarks or registered trademarks of Callisto Media Inc. and/or its affiliates, in the United States and other countries, and may not be used without written permission. All other trademarks are the property of their respective owners. Rockridge Press is not associated with any product or vendor mentioned in this book.

Series Designer: Tricia Jang
Interior and Cover Designer: Tricia Jang
Art Producer: Samantha Ulban
Editor: Mary Colgan
Production Editor: Nora Milman
Production Manager: Sandy Noman

Illustrations © 2022 Cait Brennan.
Author Photo Courtesy of © Rebecca Palmer.

Paperback ISBN: 978-1-63878-147-9
eBook ISBN: 978-1-63878-277-3
R0

For all my girls:
lab partners, research collaborators,
colleagues, mothers, daughters, friends,
mentors, and especially my students.
Thank you for co-creating our place of
belonging in the world of STEM.

CONTENTS

INTRODUCTION

Welcome to *Adventure Girls! STEM Crafts!* I'm so excited to build and create with you. Since I was a girl, I've loved all kinds of crafty pursuits, from sewing to woodworking to jewelry making. Now that I'm an adult, I work as a science, technology, engineering, and mathematics (STEM) teacher. I coach middle school LEGO League and high school robotics. I also teach middle school and high school classes in science and agriculture. Every day, I notice how under-standing STEM empowers my students to be courageously curious: They learn how to find answers to questions that have never been asked before, which means that they are ready to solve the problems of the future.

I've written this book to help girls like you develop a love of building and creating, and to encourage you to be adventurous, creative, and strong. As you read this book, you can expect to find fun, bold ways to develop your STEM skills. I hope that as you discover the secrets of the STEM universe, you also discover what a cool, capable person you are.

THE WORLD NEEDS ADVENTURE GIRLS LIKE YOU TO LEAD THE WAY!

ON THE MOVE

Understanding what affects motion is important for Adventure Girls because we build gadgets that move. By building toys, you'll learn about how the energy of motion can be transferred and how stored energy can be used to spin a color wheel and propel small objects.

NEWTON'S BOUNCE

Newton's cradle is a device that shows how energy can be transferred from one object to other objects. For this activity, you will build your own Newton's cradle.

WHAT YOU'LL NEED

- ☐ 1 sturdy sewing needle
- ☐ 5 pieces of fishing line, each 2 feet long
- ☐ 5 bouncy balls (all the same size)
- ☐ Needle-nose pliers
- ☐ Clear or masking tape
- ☐ Shoebox

1. Ask an adult to use the sturdy needle to thread a 2-foot piece of fishing line through each bouncy ball. If the needle gets stuck in the ball, use the needle-nose pliers to pull it through.

2. Tape the ends of the 5 pieces of line, one at a time, to the opposite sides of the shoebox. The bouncy balls should line up next to one another down the center of the box, with no space between the balls.

STEP 1

STEP 2

> ⇒*FUN TIP*⇐ Try designing a Newton's cradle that keeps moving longer by using a heavier material, like glass beads.

CONTINUED →

3. If you need to adjust the height of the bouncy balls, pull gently on the fishing line without moving the tape.

4. Lift the ball on one end up high, then let it go. What happens to the ball at the other end?

STEP 4

THE PHYSICS OF TOYS

Toys offer great ways to explore motion. Different materials move differently because gravity has a different effect depending on the weight of the material. Toys made of heavy-metal materials will move differently from plastic or wooden toys. Newton's cradles are usually built using metal balls because heavy materials transfer motion better than light materials.

ILLUSION TWIRLER

When we look at an object in motion, our eyes see a combination of colors on the object! You can create this illusion yourself with some simple materials.

WHAT YOU'LL NEED

- ☐ Markers
- ☐ Round object, 3 to 5 inches across
- ☐ Cardboard or empty cereal box
- ☐ Scissors
- ☐ Glue
- ☐ Yarn needle
- ☐ Piece of yarn, 5 feet long

1. Using a marker and a round object 3 to 5 inches across, trace 3 circles on the cardboard.

2. Cut out the circles with scissors.

3. Glue the circles in a stack.

STEP 3

4. Decorate the cardboard circle stack on both sides using patterns and a variety of colors. For example, you could divide the circle into 8 pie wedges and color each wedge a different amount or a different color.

STEP 4

5. Punch 2 holes, about a half inch apart, in the center of the cardboard circle with the yarn needle.

CONTINUED →

6. Thread the 5-foot piece of yarn up through one hole and down through the other, then tie the ends to create a loop.

7. Hold one end of the loop in each hand loosely with the cardboard circle in the middle. Twirl one end of the yarn loop to twist the yarn.

8. Stretch the yarn loop tight by moving your arms apart. Watch the cardboard circle as it spins. Do you see separate colors or a combination of colors?

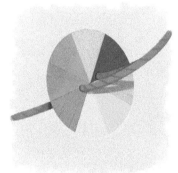

STEP 6

STEP 8

PARTY POPPER

Everyone loves party prizes! For this craft, you will power an explosion by snapping a stretched balloon and shooting goodies into the air.

WHAT YOU'LL NEED

- ☐ Scissors
- ☐ 1 (8.5-by-11 inch) sheet of cardstock
- ☐ Masking tape
- ☐ Markers
- ☐ 1 balloon
- ☐ Small toys, wrapped candy, confetti, or kind messages written on small slips of paper

1. With scissors, cut the cardstock in half and set one half aside for a future project. Decorate the other half with markers.

2. Roll the cardstock into a tube and secure it with masking tape.

3. Tie the open end of the balloon into a knot.

4. Cut off the top of the tied balloon.

5. Stretch the tied portion of the balloon over one end of the tube.

6. Fill the tube about one-quarter full with goodies—small toys, wrapped candy, confetti, or kind messages written on small pieces of paper.

STEP 1

STEP 5

CONTINUED →

7. With the open end of the tube pointing up and away from your body, pull the balloon knot down, then let it go with a snap. The motion of the balloon snapping back into place will push the popper goodies out the other end. Your party popper will pop whatever is inside it in a shower of fun!

STEP 7

ADVENTURE GIRL CHALLENGE

Experiment with how you pack your popper and how you snap the balloon to see how far you can get the confetti to go.

SPLISH SPLASH!

On Earth, water can be a liquid, solid (ice), or gas (steam). In this section, you will build a sprinkler to study liquid under pressure and a device for observing the water cycle. Check out the Adventure Girl Challenge to explore one of the most interesting properties of solid water: Ice floats!

SUPER SPRINKLER

Liquid water takes the shape of its container—and squirts out when there's enough pressure. Let's have some fun and get wet!

WHAT YOU'LL NEED

- ☐ 1 bamboo skewer
- ☐ 1 foam pool noodle
- ☐ Garden hose, hooked up to a water supply
- ☐ Duct tape

1. Use the bamboo skewer to poke about 20 holes through the foam pool noodle.

2. Attach a garden hose to one end of the pool noodle.

3. Use duct tape to cover the open end of the pool noodle.

4. Set your pool noodle on the ground.

5. Turn on the water and enjoy your noodle sprinkler!

STEP 1

STEPS 2 & 3

> ⇒*FUN TIP*⇐ Try connecting 3 or 4 pool noodles in a loop for a new sprinkler shape!

WINDOW WATER CYCLE

For this activity, you're going to build a simple device that will let you observe several steps in the water cycle: evaporation, condensation, precipitation, and percolation.

WHAT YOU'LL NEED

- ☐ 5 to 10 cotton balls
- ☐ 1 quart-size zip-top bag
- ☐ ¼ cup of water
- ☐ 3 drops of blue food coloring
- ☐ Painter's tape

1. Place the cotton balls in a single row along the bottom of the zip-top bag.

2. Add 3 drops of food coloring to a cup holding ¼ cup of water.

3. Pour the water into the bag and zip it closed.

STEP 1

4. Use painter's tape to secure the bag to a sunny window.

5. Check your bag every 30 minutes until you see fog on the plastic. This is condensation, the part of the water cycle when evaporated water changes from gas to liquid and forms clouds.

6. Eventually, you will see drops of water sliding down the plastic. This is like precipitation, the part of the water cycle when condensed water falls down as rain.

7. When the droplets reach the cotton balls, this is percolation, the part of the water cycle when rain sinks down into the ground.

STEP 7

WATER: THE SECRET TO LIFE

Life is possible on Earth because water can be a solid, liquid, or gas. When water moves through the water cycle, rain reaches the whole planet. Without the water cycle, Earth would just be a desert and an ocean! Water can also dissolve the chemicals needed for living things to survive, like sugar and salt.

ADVENTURE GIRL CHALLENGE

For almost every substance in the universe, the solid form sinks in liquid. But not water! Make an ice boat: Thoroughly soak a small sponge and place it in a plastic container. Place the container in the freezer for 2 hours. Take the icy sponge out of the container and place it in a sink full of water—it floats!

MEASURE THIS!

A famous saying among builders is "Measure twice, cut once." The focus of this section is on taking measurements and recording and studying data—key skills for builders like you!

DESIGN TO SCALE

Building a scale model of a room makes it much easier to design your dream room. Bonus: Arranging the furniture doesn't require any heavy lifting.

WHAT YOU'LL NEED

- ☐ Tape measure
- ☐ Graph paper
- ☐ Pencil
- ☐ Scissors
- ☐ Clear or double-sided tape (optional)

1. Choose a room to model, such as your bedroom or living room.

2. Measure the length and width of a piece of furniture in feet. If the furniture is up to 5 inches over a particular foot measurement, round up to the nearest half foot (for example, 3 feet 4 inches becomes 3 ½ feet). If the furniture is 6 to 11 inches over a particular foot measurement, round up to the nearest whole foot (3 feet 8 inches becomes 4 feet).

DRAWING TO SCALE

Scale drawings are super-important tools in building projects. Whenever a house is built or remodeled, an architect creates scale blueprints with every detail of the project included. Builders keep the blueprints next to them as they measure, cut, and put together the wood and other materials of the house.

CONTINUED →

DESIGN TO SCALE CONTINUED

3. On a sheet of graph paper, draw a shape representing your furniture. Use one square on the graph paper for each foot. For example, if your bed is 6 feet long and 3 feet wide, draw a rectangle 6 squares by 3 squares. Label the shape with the name of the piece of furniture you measured.

4. Repeat steps 1, 2, and 3 with the rest of the furniture in the room.

STEP 4

5. Now measure the room itself, rounding up its measurements as you did with the furniture. Trace a scale outline of the room on a second sheet of graph paper. Mark the locations of windows and doors.

6. With scissors, cut out the furniture shapes and place them on the room outline. If you want, attach them lightly with a loop of clear tape or double-sided tape.

STEP 5

STEP 6

CONTINUED →

7. Try moving the furniture shapes around to create different arrangements. You can add other furniture to make a dream room just as fun and imaginative as you are. Have fun designing your room with your scale model!

STEP 7

NATURE GRAPH

Nature comes in a variety of shapes and sizes. For this activity, you will practice measuring and recording data using natural objects.

WHAT YOU'LL NEED

- ☐ An outdoor space where flowers, fruits, seeds, leaves, sticks, and/or rocks can be collected
- ☐ Ruler
- ☐ Graph paper
- ☐ Pencil
- ☐ Glue
- ☐ Colored pencils

1. Go outside and collect 10 items in nature, such as seeds, fruits, flowers, leaves, sticks, and rocks. Try to get items of different heights.

2. Lay the items on a flat surface next to a ruler. Make sure the items line up at the bottom.

STEP 2

3. Use the ruler to measure the height of each item in inches. Write the measurements on the back of a piece of graph paper.

4. On the front side of the graph paper, draw a graph. Label the y-axis "height (in inches)." On the x-axis, group the items by type (for example, fruits, flowers, and sticks).

CONTINUED →

STEP 5

5. Draw a bar on the graph to represent the height of each item measured. Remember to draw the bars for fruits in one group, for flowers in another, and so on.

6. Turn your graph into a piece of art by gluing your nature items next to their bars. Decorate the page with colored pencil drawings.

> *⇒FUN TIP⇐* Try arranging natural items in a vase or cup with some water or sand. Notice how items of different heights look when they are gathered together. The arrangement in your vase could make a nice decoration for your room or a gift for someone special!

ADVENTURE GIRL CHALLENGE

Measure, record, and graph different kinds of data. For example, ask 10 people about their favorite types of movies and make a graph to show what you learned.

OUTER SPACE

There's nothing quite like outer space to ignite the imagination. What was it like to fly to the Moon? Will humans ever travel to Mars? Fire up your spirit of adventure as you build a telescope, chart stars and planets in a sky journal, and blast off a rocket.

HOMEMADE TELESCOPE

Have you ever wanted to see the surface of the Moon or the colors of stars? With this homemade telescope, you can zoom in to study objects in the night sky!

⚠ **CAUTION:** Have an adult do all the steps involving the X-Acto knife and spray paint. Wear gloves when working with an X-Acto knife. Wear goggles and a face mask when working with spray paint.

1. Use a Sharpie marker to draw a line around 2 (2-liter) plastic bottles, about 2 inches from the bottom.

2. Have an adult use an X-Acto knife to cut along the lines.

3. Set the 1- or 2-inch convex magnifying lens on top of one of the 2-liter bottles. If the lens hangs over the edge by more than ¼ inch, you will need to have an adult trim off part of the bottleneck to get a better fit. This will be the top piece of your telescope.

CONTINUED →

4. Draw a circle around the other bottle at the base of the neck. Have an adult cut off this part of the bottle to make a cylinder. This will be the bottom piece of your telescope.

5. Place both trimmed bottles in a cardboard box outdoors. Have an adult paint the bottles with black spray paint.

6. Place the 4-inch magnifying glass with a handle on top of the cylinder and attach it with electrical tape.

7. Place the 1- to 2-inch convex magnifying lens on top of the top piece of the telescope and attach it with electrical tape.

8. Slide the cylinder piece inside the top piece to complete your telescope. Look through the smaller lens to see a faraway object appear larger and closer.

TOP

BOTTOM

STEP 4

STEPS 6 & 7

STEP 8

NIGHT SKY JOURNAL

Track the Moon, stars, planets, and other nighttime sky wonders in this awesome journaling activity!

WHAT YOU'LL NEED

- ☐ Flashlight
- ☐ Brown paper lunch bag
- ☐ Notebook
- ☐ Pencil
- ☐ Compass (optional)
- ☐ Star chart or stargazing app (optional)
- ☐ Crayons, colored pencils, or markers (optional)

1. Prepare to observe the night sky by making a night-friendly light. Slide a flashlight into a brown paper lunch bag. Turn on the flashlight and shine it down on the ground. This dim light will provide enough light for you to write but won't make it difficult to see in the dark.

2. Go outside with an adult and bring the flashlight, notebook, and pencil. Try to find an area without many bright lights, trees, or tall buildings.

3. Open your notebook and write down the date and time, then draw a circle to represent your view of the horizon in all directions.

4. If you have a compass, mark north on your sky circle.

5. Draw any trees or buildings that surround your view.

CONTINUED →

NIGHT SKY JOURNAL CONTINUED

New Moon | Waxing Crescent | First Quarter | Waxing Gibbous | Full Moon | Waning Gibbous | Third Quarter | Waning Crescent

6. Draw the Moon in the sky, marking which phase it is in. Use the chart on this page as a guide.

7. Draw the stars and constellations you see. If you have a star chart or stargazing app, you can use it to add labels.

8. If you see a very bright star, it could be a planet! Mark this down.

9. If you see a quickly moving object, it could be a satellite! Mark this down.

10. Try to go outside every night. Notice how the Moon phase changes over time. If you see colors in the night sky, add color to your journal.

BLASTOFF!

Use the explosive power of a chemical reaction to launch a rocket high in the sky!

WHAT YOU'LL NEED

- ☐ 1 cork that fits the bottle
- ☐ 1 empty (2-liter) plastic bottle
- ☐ Painter's tape
- ☐ 4 chopsticks
- ☐ Duct tape
- ☐ 2 cups of vinegar
- ☐ ⅛ cup of baking soda
- ☐ Wax paper

⚠ *CAUTION:* Safety goggles and gloves are recommended for this activity. The vinegar will splash.

1. Put the cork in the plastic bottle to make sure that it fits snugly. Then remove it.

2. Use painter's tape to attach 4 chopsticks to the bottle to form a stand.

3. Once the chopsticks are positioned correctly, use duct tape to secure them in place.

STEP 3

4. Pour 2 cups of vinegar into the bottle.

5. Pour ⅛ cup of baking soda onto a piece of wax paper.

CONTINUED →

6. Take the bottle, baking soda, and cork out-side. Set the bottle on a flat surface with the bottle neck pointing up. Bend the wax paper into a U-shape and quickly pour the baking soda into the bottle and insert the cork. Hold the cork firmly in place as you turn the bottle upside down.

7. Remove the cork and step away from the rocket as it lifts off the ground!

STEP 6

⇒*FUN TIP*⇐ Try decorating your rocket with colorful markers or adding food coloring to the vinegar.

ADVENTURE GIRL CHALLENGE

Experiment with different amounts of vinegar and baking soda to make your bottle rocket fly higher.

MAE C. JEMISON

(1956–)

is a medical doctor, engineer, and astronaut. Jemison is famous for becoming the first African American woman to travel to space on an 8-day mission in 1992, but she has also served as a doctor in the Peace Corps, advocated for social change and bringing technology to developing countries, and taught environmental studies. She is an international leader in space travel, education, and science.

BUILD THIS!

Building and construction challenges are fun to tackle because you get to think your way to a solution you can see and touch. This section involves building structures that will collapse over and over—until you figure out your solutions. If your building falls, don't give up—build it again!

HOUSE OF CARDS

A house of cards looks simple, but it can be very tricky to build. The key is to begin with a very stable base. (If the base isn't stable, you can literally blow the house down!)

WHAT YOU'LL NEED

- ☐ 15 playing cards
- ☐ Placemat (optional)

1. Carefully place 2 playing cards in a triangle shape with their top edges touching. A non-slip base surface, like a placemat, will make your house of cards less likely to collapse. Remember, if your cards fall down, don't give up! This is frustrating but normal. It takes lots of practice to build a stable truss, or triangle-shaped building support.

2. Repeat step 1 until you have 3 triangular trusses made of 6 cards in all.

3. Gently place 2 cards flat across your trusses to create a roof.

4. Carefully build 2 more trusses on top of this roof.

5. Place 1 card on the 2 new trusses to create a second roof.

6. Build 1 final truss out of 2 cards to make the top of your house of cards.

SKYSCRAPER CHALLENGE

Use foam circles and toothpicks to design and build a tower that reaches to the sky!

WHAT YOU'LL NEED

- ☐ Scissors
- ☐ Ruler
- ☐ 1 foam pool noodle
- ☐ 1 box of toothpicks

1. Use scissors and the ruler to cut the foam pool noodle into 1-inch circle pieces. You might need to ask an adult to help.

2. Stick a toothpick into a foam circle as shown. The toothpick is going to work as a stud, which is a vertical support used in building construction.

STEP 1

3. Use several toothpick studs to connect one foam circle to the next as you build the stories of your skyscraper. Try using different numbers of toothpicks. Try changing the positions of the toothpicks. What is the most stable arrangement of toothpick studs?

STEP 2

STEP 3

4. How high can you build your skyscraper? Engineer the tallest skyscraper that you can (that stands up on its own!).

> ⋛*FUN TIP*⋚ Have a contest with a friend to see who can build the tallest skyscraper.

THE HISTORY OF TRUSSES

Trusses, or triangle-shaped building supports, were probably first used in the Bronze Age, over 4,500 years ago. Trusses were popular in the United States for building railroad bridges during the 1800s, when trains traveled across the North American continent. Early bridges were made of wood, but by the mid-1800s many bridges were built of metal and stone.

ADVENTURE GIRL CHALLENGE

Design and build a skyscraper that will hold some weight. How many books can you balance on your skyscraper before it falls down?

MATH MOSAICS

Math can be beautiful when you bring it to life using materials you can see and touch! In this section, you will practice multiplication, which is adding equal groups of numbers, with two fun hands-on activities.

TERRIFIC TESSELLATIONS

A tessellation is a repeating pattern of shapes. To make a tessellation, you will multiply a single shape many times.

WHAT YOU'LL NEED

- ☐ Scissors
- ☐ Empty cereal box or 1 sheet of cardstock
- ☐ Pencil
- ☐ Clear tape
- ☐ Paper
- ☐ Markers, crayons, or colored pencils

1. Use scissors to cut a small square of cardstock, about 2 inches by 2 inches, from an empty cereal box or sheet of cardstock.

2. Draw a line down the center of the cardstock with curves, shapes, or zigzags to make it interesting. (Don't draw a straight line.)

3. Cut along the line you drew.

STEP 3

4. Rotate the 2 pieces and tape the 2 straight sides together, back-to-back.

5. Draw another interesting line across the middle of the taped pieces of cardstock, between the two non-straight edges.

STEP 4

CONTINUED →

6. Cut along the second line, rotate the pieces, and tape them back-to-back along the straight edges.

7. Now it's time to multiply (add equal groups to) your tessellation. Use a pencil to trace the cardstock shape on a piece of paper. Then move the cardstock so that it fits just above your tracing, like a puzzle piece. Trace it again. Repeat until you fill the page.

8. Use markers, crayons, or colored pencils to color in your tessellations.

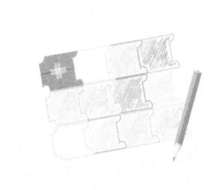

> ⇒**FUN TIP**⇐ Can you make a tessellation that looks like an animal? Try drawing lines of different styles until you get a tessellation shape that you love.

MARBLE MOSAIC

In this activity, you will use multiplication to create mosaics, which are patterns of organized small objects.

WHAT YOU'LL NEED

- ☐ Flat marbles, glass gems, or beads
- ☐ 3 or 4 sheets of paper
- ☐ Pencil

1. Line up 3 rows of 2 marbles each on a sheet of paper.

2. Use a pencil to mark rows 1, 2, and 3.

3. Use a pencil to mark columns 1 and 2.

4. Use a pencil to mark marbles 1, 2, 3, 4, 5, and 6.

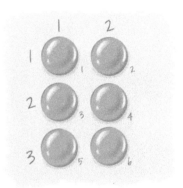

STEPS 1 - 4

5. Write the math sentence that represents your marbles: 2 × 3 = 6.

6. Repeat with a different number of marbles as many times as you like. When you write your math sentence, you can put the columns number or the rows number first. Challenge yourself to create math sentences that are new or more difficult.

CONTINUED →

THE HISTORY OF MOSAICS

Mosaics are an ancient art form. For thousands of years, people have used shells, pebbles, bone, and tile to create mosaics on the floors, ceilings, and walls of homes and sacred spaces. Although many mosaics are shaped-based patterns, others are depictions of myths, religious stories, animals, and beautiful places.

ADVENTURE GIRL CHALLENGE

Once you have mastered marble mosaics, design a mosaic that makes a pattern or picture and glue it to paper to create a work of art.

CROSS THAT BRIDGE

There are some amazing forces involved in getting a bridge to work safely! Arches, beams, and cables are just a few of the technologies used to suspend bridges from their anchorages. In this section, you will create a castle drawbridge and engineer beam, truss, and suspension bridges from paper.

UPCYCLED DRAWBRIDGE

Reuse everyday materials to build a working drawbridge!

WHAT YOU'LL NEED

- ☐ Markers
- ☐ Empty cereal box
- ☐ Ruler
- ☐ Scissors
- ☐ Paper
- ☐ Clear tape
- ☐ Hole punch
- ☐ String

1. With a marker, draw 2 lines, about 4 inches apart, down the front of a cereal box. Use the ruler to guide the marker and keep the lines straight.

2. Use scissors to cut down the lines to make the drawbridge.

STEP 2

3. Open your drawbridge and wrap a sheet of paper around it. Secure the paper with tape.

4. Use markers to decorate the paper on the front of your drawbridge to look like the front of a castle.

STEP 3

5. Use a hole punch to make 2 holes at the top of the drawbridge and 2 holes at the top of the back of the cereal box.

CONTINUED →

6. Cut a 3-foot piece of string. Thread it through the left drawbridge hole. Tie the string.

7. Thread the string through the left hole at the back of the box, from the inside of the box going out.

8. Bring the string through the right hole at the back of the box from the outside in.

9. Thread the string through the right drawbridge hole and tie the string.

10. To close the drawbridge, pull the string loop at the back of the box. To open the drawbridge, let the string go.

STEPS 6 – 8

STEP 10

ADVENTURE GIRL CHALLENGE

Try building a castle with a drawbridge outside with materials you find in nature, like sticks, rocks, and leaves. Dig a moat around your castle and fill it with water.

ONE-DOLLAR BRIDGE

Design and build a paper bridge that can hold up one dollar in nickels, dimes, or quarters!

WHAT YOU'LL NEED

- ☐ 10 sheets of paper
- ☐ Markers
- ☐ 2 large books that are equally thick
- ☐ Clean, empty yogurt cup
- ☐ Scissors
- ☐ Clear tape
- ☐ 10 dimes
- ☐ 4 quarters
- ☐ 20 nickels

1. Fold 1 sheet of paper in half lengthwise and draw a road on it with markers.

2. Position the 2 large books 7 inches apart and place the road on top to make a bridge.

STEP 2

3. Put the yogurt cup on top of the bridge and watch what happens. This bridge needs support!

4. To make a beam bridge, use scissors to cut 3 strips of paper that are as wide as the books are tall. Roll each strip into a column, secure with tape, and place under the bridge.

5. To make a truss bridge, accordion-fold a piece of paper and place it under the bridge.

STEP 5

CONTINUED →

6. To build a suspension bridge, roll 2 sheets of paper to make tall columns. Use long strips of paper, folded 3 times for added thickness, to connect the columns to the bridge. Secure the strips with tape.

STEP 6

7. Test the strength of each bridge by putting one dollar in coins inside the yogurt cup and placing the cup on the bridge. Medium-strength bridges will hold up 10 dimes. Strong bridges will hold up 4 quarters. Extra-strong bridges will hold up 20 nickels.

> *≥FUN TIP≤* Try building your bridge using cardstock instead of paper. Can it hold 100 pennies?

STICKS AND STONES: EARLY BRIDGES

The earliest-known types of bridges were stepping-stones, boardwalks, and log bridges. Stones let people cross rivers by stepping from stone to stone across the water. Boardwalks are walkways built over wet or marshy areas that provide a dry path. Log bridges are made from cut trees that are long enough to reach from one edge of a river or chasm to the other.

UP IN THE AIR

Planes can fly because air lifts them up. When the movement of air over a plane wing is faster than the movement of air under it, the pressure difference creates a force that lifts the plane. Air might be invisible, but it's powerful enough to lift kites, bubbles, and even balls!

LET'S BUILD A KITE!

Build your own kite and watch it soar above the trees!

WHAT YOU'LL NEED

- ☐ Scissors
- ☐ 3 bamboo skewers with the pointy tips cut off
- ☐ String
- ☐ 1 sheet of newspaper
- ☐ Masking tape
- ☐ 1 kite string with holder

1. With scissors, cut 1 of the bamboo skewers in half. Cross the 2 long bamboo skewers near the ends to make a corner shape and firmly tie them together with string.

2. Place the skewers on a piece of newspaper with the tied ends at the top.

STEPS 1 & 2

3. Use tape to secure the tied skewers to the newspaper, at the tied top and at the two untied ends.

4. Trim the newspaper so that there is a 1-inch border along the outside of the skewers.

STEPS 3 & 4

CONTINUED →

5. Fold the newspaper border over the skewers and tape it down.

6. Place 1 half of a skewer on your kite so that it runs across the kite, touching both side skewers. Tape it down at the edges.

7. Clip or tie the kite string to the center of the half skewer and secure it with tape.

8. Take your kite outside and let it fly!

STEPS 5 & 6

ADVENTURE GIRL CHALLENGE

Teach a friend how to build a kite and fly your kites together. Notice whose kite stays up longer and try to figure out why. Work together to design a new kite that stays up even longer!

FLOATING ON AIR

When air moves, it can lift heavy objects—even airplanes! It's pretty hard to bring an airplane home to work with, so you'll experiment with lift using a Ping-Pong ball.

WHAT YOU'LL NEED

- ☐ Hair dryer
- ☐ Ping-Pong ball

1. Plug in a hair dryer, point it straight up, and turn it on.

2. Hold a Ping-Pong ball directly over the flow of air coming from the hair dryer.

3. Slowly let go of the ball. What happens?

STEP 1

FLORENCE LOWE "PANCHO" BARNES

(1901–1975)

was the first female Hollywood stunt pilot. In 1930s movies with dangerous airplane scenes, she flew so that famous actors didn't have to take risks. Pancho stood up for fair pay and safety for stunt pilots in Hollywood and ran training programs that supported female pilots.

BUBBLE CLOUDS

Bubbles are mostly air, are very light, and float easily. Make huge clouds of bubbles outside and watch them float away with the wind!

WHAT YOU'LL NEED

- ☐ Scissors
- ☐ 12-ounce plastic water bottle, empty, with no cap
- ☐ Clean sock
- ☐ Rubber band
- ☐ 1 small bottle of bubble solution
- ☐ Bowl
- ☐ A windy day

⚠ **CAUTION:** Have an adult do the step involving the scissors.

1. Have an adult use scissors to cut the bottom off the plastic water bottle.

2. Stretch the sock over the open bottom of the water bottle. If the sock is longer than the bottle, fold it over to make it fit. Secure it in place with a rubber band.

STEPS 1 & 2

3. Pour the bottle of bubble solution into the bowl.

4. Bring your sock bottle and bubble solution outside on a windy day.

CONTINUED →

5. Holding on to the top of the water bottle, dip the bottom of it, with the sock, into the bowl of bubble solution.

6. Blow through the top of the bottle to make a huge cloud of bubbles. Watch the wind carry your bubble cloud up, up, and away!

STEP 5

⇒ *FUN TIP* ⇐ Try adding food coloring to your bubble solution to make rainbow bubble clouds.

STUCK ON YOU

Electromagnetism, the force of nature involving electricity and magnets, is all around us. All materials make magnetic fields, but in most objects many tiny magnetic fields point in different directions, canceling each other out. In magnets, all of the fields line up and the electromagnetic force can actually be detected. When Adventure Girls understand how magnets work, we can harness their electromagnetic force as we build!

MAGNETIC PHOTOS

Lots of people set pictures they like in picture frames. But you're an Adventure Girl! You're going to use electromagnetic force to display your favorite photo.

WHAT YOU'LL NEED

- ☐ Canning jar lid, without the ring
- ☐ Photo, at least 3 inches by 3 inches in size
- ☐ Pencil
- ☐ Scissors
- ☐ Glue
- ☐ Small paintbrush
- ☐ Mod Podge (finishing glue)
- ☐ Plastic gems, beads, or other decorations
- ☐ Small magnet

1. Place the canning jar lid on top of the photo over your favorite part. Trace the lid with a pencil. Use scissors to cut out the circle you traced.

2. Glue the photo to the nonmetal side of the lid.

3. Use the small paintbrush to paint the photo with Mod Podge and allow it to dry.

4. Once the Mod Podge has dried, decorate the edge of the photo by gluing down plastic gems or beads. Allow the glue to dry.

5. Once the glue is dry, flip the photo over.

6. Use glue to attach the small magnet to the metal side of the lid. The magnet will click onto the lid, and the glue will keep the magnet in place. Allow the glue to dry.

7. Display your magnetic photo on your refrigerator for everyone in your family to see!

CONTINUED →

> ⇒*FUN TIP*⇐ Make a set of photo magnets and give them to a special friend as a gift.

EARTH'S MAGNETIC FIELD

Our home planet is a magnet! Part of Earth's core has electric currents that generate a huge magnetic field. Migrating animals, including sea turtles, fish, lobsters, and birds, can sense Earth's magnetic field. This may be how older sea turtles find and return to the beaches where they hatched as babies.

I CAN'T LEGO!

For this activity, you will pit electromagnetic force against buoyancy—the force that makes objects float. Let the battle begin!

WHAT YOU'LL NEED

- ☐ Newspaper
- ☐ 1 LEGO minifigure
- ☐ Flat magnet
- ☐ Sharpie marker
- ☐ Scissors
- ☐ Waterproof glue, such as Gorilla Kids School Glue
- ☐ Small bowl
- ☐ Water
- ☐ 10 small paper clips

1. Lay down a sheet of newspaper to make a workspace.

2. Stand the LEGO minifigure on the magnet and trace its feet with a Sharpie marker.

3. Use scissors to cut out your tracing. You should have a small rectangular magnet.

4. Lay the magnet with the black part facing down.

5. Carefully put waterproof glue on the LEGO minifigure's feet. Turn the LEGO minifigure right-side up and set its feet firmly on the magnet. Leave the glue to dry according to the package directions.

STEP 5

CONTINUED →

6. Once the glue has dried, fill the small bowl with water. Put the LEGO minifigure and one paper clip in the water. Do they sink or float?

7. Take the LEGO minifigure and paper clip out of the water. Touch the magnet to the paper clip so it sticks. Place the LEGO minifigure with the attached paper clip in the water. Does it float or sink?

STEP 6

8. Make a chain of 2 paper clips by linking them together. Touch the magnet to the paper clips so they stick. Does the LEGO minifigure float or sink?

9. Keep adding paper clips to the chain until the LEGO minifigure sinks. How many paper clips are needed to overcome the force of buoyancy?

STEP 9

ADVENTURE GIRL CHALLENGE

Use a magnet to push or pull a metal toy car. Organize a magnetic mini-car race with a friend.

REAL REACTIONS

Chemistry is the science of matter, or all the materials that make up the universe. Chemistry helps us understand how certain substances react with one another to make new (and sometimes surprising!) substances. In this section, you will combine materials to create chemical reactions in a craft that uses a reaction to create art and an activity that demonstrates a basic principle of substances reacting.

FIZZ ART

Alka-Seltzer is a chemical that combines with water to make gas bubbles. Painting with Alka-Seltzer makes art that literally pops off the page!

WHAT YOU'LL NEED

- 6 Alka-Seltzer tablets
- Zip-top bag
- Toy hammer or any tool that can be used to crush Alka-Seltzer
- 1 sheet of watercolor paper
- 6 paper towels
- Food coloring
- Plastic cup with ⅛ cup of water
- Plastic pipette or dropper

1. Place the 6 Alka-Seltzer tablets in a zip-top bag. Use a toy hammer (or other safe tool) to crush the tablets.

2. Place 1 sheet of watercolor paper on top of a thick layer of paper towels. Make sure that the towels extend beyond the edges of the paper.

STEP 1

3. Sprinkle the crushed Alka-Seltzer over the watercolor paper. Remove any large chunks of Alka-Seltzer.

4. Add 4 drops of food coloring to ⅛ cup of water in a plastic cup.

5. Use a plastic pipette or dropper to drip the colorful water onto the Alka-Seltzer powder on the watercolor paper.

CONTINUED →

FIZZ ART CONTINUED

6. Continue painting with the colorful water. Add a second color when you are ready. Keep an eye on where the water goes. The colorful water may drip off the sides of the watercolor paper and onto the paper towels.

7. Let your artwork dry, then scrape off any uncolored Alka-Seltzer powder.

8. Display your artwork as a keepsake!

STEP 5

>*FUN TIP*< Try making fizz art with baking powder instead of Alka-Seltzer. Paint with colorful vinegar to make lots of bubbles!

ADVENTURE GIRL CHALLENGE

Help an adult make pancakes and look for evidence of chemical reactions. Bubbles, color changes, and strong smells are key signs of substances reacting.

MYSTERY EGG

When baking soda and vinegar combine, they make a big, bubbly chemical reaction. In this activity, you will make a baking soda egg and dissolve it with vinegar. No need to crack this egg!

WHAT YOU'LL NEED

- ☐ ½ cup of baking soda
- ☐ 1 small bowl
- ☐ Yellow and red food coloring
- ☐ Spoon
- ☐ 1 tablespoon of water, plus 1 to 2 teaspoons
- ☐ Small plastic toy
- ☐ 1 large, clear plastic food storage container
- ☐ 1 cup of vinegar

1. Place the ½ cup of baking soda in a small bowl.

2. Add 5 drops of yellow food coloring and 3 drops of red food coloring.

3. Stir together with the spoon. The baking soda will still look mostly white.

4. Add 1 tablespoon of water and stir the mixture thoroughly.

5. Reach into the bowl and squeeze a handful of baking soda. If it sticks together like putty, you are ready to make your egg. If it does not stick together, add another 1 to 2 teaspoons of water until it feels like dry Play-Doh.

6. Squeeze a handful of the dyed baking soda into a ball, then press the small toy inside it.

STEP 6

CONTINUED →

7. Press more baking soda on top of the toy until it is completely covered.

8. Place the mystery egg in the large, clear plastic food storage container.

9. Slowly pour 1 cup of vinegar over the egg and enjoy the wild chemical reaction!

STEP 9

ENVIRONMENTAL CHEMICAL ENGINEERING

Chemical engineers often team up with environmental scientists to protect our water, air, soil, and wildlife. For example, chemical engineers have helped develop tiny bacteria that can break down pollution in water and soil. Junkyards, fertilizer spills, and oil spills have all been cleaned up with these miraculous microbes.

NATURAL DISASTERS

Natural disasters are big, destructive weather events, like floods, hurricanes, and earthquakes. The first step in being ready for natural disasters is understanding how and why they happen. Let's build a bottle tornado to see how tornados form and create a tiny tsunami to show how big ocean waves lead to flooding.

TORNADO IN A BOTTLE

Tornados form when clouds are pulled by both the circular motion of swirling winds and gravity's downward force. In this craft, as water drains from one bottle to another, you'll see the same motion happening.

WHAT YOU'LL NEED

- ☐ 2 (2-liter) bottles
- ☐ Water
- ☐ Blue food coloring
- ☐ 1-inch washer with ⅜-inch opening
- ☐ 2 pieces of duct tape, one 12 inches and one 6 inches in length

1. Fill one of the 2-liter bottles three-quarters full of water.

2. Add 1 drop of blue food coloring to the water.

3. Place the 1-inch washer over the top of the bottle with water in it. The washer should be large enough to rest on top of the bottle without falling in.

4. Flip the empty 2-liter bottle upside down and place it exactly over the full bottle. Line up the bottle necks and openings.

5. Use the 12-inch piece of duct tape to tape the bottles together. Cover both bottle necks completely.

STEPS 1 - 3

STEPS 4 & 5

CONTINUED →

6. Use the 6-inch piece of duct tape to add a second layer. This will secure and waterproof the connection.

7. To make a tornado, you will need to create a swirling motion in the water as it drains downward. Holding the duct taped bottle heads firmly, flip the entire gadget over, then move your hand in a circular motion.

STEP 7

8. Set your gadget down and watch the tornado form.

9. Practice makes perfect! Keep flipping and swirling your tornado bottle until you can confidently create a model storm.

PREPARING FOR NATURAL DISASTERS

Hopefully you won't ever experience a natural disaster, but there are some safety plans you can make just in case. Talk with your family about the safest place to shelter in your home if severe weather arrives. Know how to tune in to weather reports to find out if a storm is coming. Keep the batteries in your flashlight fresh in case of an electrical outage.

TINY TSUNAMI

Tsunamis are giant ocean waves caused by earthquakes. In this activity, you will make a model of a shoreline and watch a tsunami start a flood.

WHAT YOU'LL NEED

- ☐ 1 sheet of paper
- ☐ 1-liter plastic bottle with a cap
- ☐ Funnel
- ☐ 1 cup of sand
- ☐ Water
- ☐ Blue food coloring

1. Roll the sheet of paper into a funnel and place it in the neck of the plastic bottle.

2. Use the funnel to pour 1 cup of sand into your bottle. The sand should be about 2 inches deep.

3. Add water to the bottle until it is half full. It is okay if the water is cloudy.

4. Add 1 drop of blue food coloring to the water. Place the cap on the bottle, making sure it is screwed on tightly.

STEP 1

STEPS 3 & 4

CONTINUED →

TINY TSUNAMI CONTINUED

5. Tip the bottle gently on its side. You will see a sloping hill of sand on the bottom end. This represents a beach, where land meets ocean.

6. Once the water is still, firmly tap the cap on the bottle using the palm of your hand. The tap represents an earthquake out at sea. A large wave will swamp the shore.

STEP 5

>⇒*FUN TIP*⇐ Try using gravel instead of sand to make the land in your tsunami model.

ADVENTURE GIRL CHALLENGE

Build a tsunami model in a large pan. Place small plastic objects and corks in the sand to see how the waves might affect houses and trees.

PATTERNS AND SHAPES

Geometry is the math of shapes, lines, and angles and is incredibly important in building. In this section, you will explore basic geometry by crafting a hexaflexagon, a folded paper that can be flexed along its folds to turn inside out. You will also practice using symmetry in building construction by creating a pop-out paper castle.

FABULOUS FLEXAGONS

Flexagons are flat shapes that can be flexed and folded to reveal hidden sides. In this craft, you will make the most basic flexagon: a 3-sided hexaflexagon.

WHAT YOU'LL NEED

- ☐ Ruler
- ☐ Pencil
- ☐ 1 sheet of paper
- ☐ Scissors
- ☐ Purple, blue, and orange markers
- ☐ Glue stick

1. Use a ruler and a pencil to draw a line 1 inch from the edge of a sheet of paper.

2. Use scissors to cut along the line to make a 1-inch strip.

3. Fold one end of the paper strip to make half of a triangle that is equilateral, meaning equal on all sides.

STEP 3

4. Fold so the bottom of the paper touches the creased edge, as shown by the arrow. Continue folding in that manner until the entire paper is made up of equilateral triangles.

STEP 4

CONTINUED →

5. Use scissors to trim the half triangle from one end and the extra paper from the other end, so that you have exactly 10 triangles.

6. Unfold the paper strip so that the left side of the strip angles in. Label the first and last triangles "glue." Color the remaining triangles in this pattern, left to right:

   (glue) • orange • purple • purple • blue • blue • orange• orange • purple • (glue)

STEP 5

7. Flip the paper strip over so that the left side of the strip angles out. Color the triangles in this pattern:

   purple • blue • blue • orange • orange • purple • purple • blue • blue • orange

STEPS 6 & 7

8. Fold the fourth triangle under the third triangle, then the seventh triangle under the sixth triangle. Lift the ninth triangle over the first triangle. You should be holding a flexagon with all blue triangles facing up.

9. Flip the hexagon over. Fold the tenth triangle over and glue the "glue" labels together so that all the upward-facing triangles are orange.

10. Pinch every other seam of your hexagon up so that the center rises out of a triangle shape. You will see a loose flap. Slip a finger into the flap and gently tug out and to the side.

11. Your entire hexaflexagon will open to another color. Repeat the triangle pinch fold and flap tug to bend your hexaflexagon into its 3 different colors!

> ⇒*FUN TIP*⇐ Try using your flexagon as a fidget. As your busy fingers fold the flexagon, take a deep breath to find calm and focus.

POP-OUT DREAM HOME

Builders usually make a model of what they are building before they begin construction. In this activity, you will learn how to use symmetrical paper cutting to build a model castle.

WHAT YOU'LL NEED

- ☐ 1 (8.5-by-11 inch) sheet of cardstock
- ☐ Markers
- ☐ Scissors
- ☐ 3 sheets of paper
- ☐ Glue stick

1. Fold the cardstock in half widthwise.

2. Unfold the cardstock and use markers to draw a landscape scene. For example, you could draw tree-covered mountains under a cloudy sky.

3. To make the first part of your castle, use scissors to cut out of a sheet of paper a rectangle about 4 inches by 6 inches. Use markers to draw rocks or bricks on the paper.

4. Fold the rectangle in half lengthwise and cut the top into a triangle shape, with the highest point of the triangle at the corner of the folded side. When you unfold the rectangle, you will see that the roof line you made is symmetrical, meaning the same on both sides.

STEPS 4 & 5

5. Fold over the long edges of the rectangle about ¼ inch. Use a glue stick to rub glue along the folds. Press the glued folds onto the cardstock to attach your castle turret to the landscape.

6. To make a battlement (a shape like the top of a castle wall), cut out a 3-by-5-inch piece of paper and fold it in half widthwise. Cut out a rectangle at the top of the folded paper, in the center. Unfold the paper, then fold the side edges over about ¼ inch. Apply glue to the folds, and adhere your battlement to your landscape next to the turret.

STEP 6

7. To make a window, cut out a 6-by-5-inch piece of paper and fold it in half length-wise. Cut a half circle out of the folded side of the paper. Unfold the paper, then fold the side edges over about ¼ inch. Apply glue to the folds, and attach the window to your landscape.

STEP 7

8. Keep experimenting with shapes by folding more small pieces of paper in half. The cutout shapes will be symmetrical if you cut through both sides of the folded paper at the same time.

CONTINUED →

9. When the walls of your castle are complete, use markers to decorate them. When you use your imagination to build your pop-out dream home, the sky's the limit!

SYMMETRY IN ARCHITECTURE

Symmetrical objects, like your hands, match perfectly when they are placed together. In architecture, symmetry can also mean balance or harmony. Symmetrical details in architecture, like the same number of windows on either side of a door, help people feel comfortable and at home in a space.

ADVENTURE GIRL CHALLENGE

Throughout the day, look around your home, at other buildings, and in nature for symmetrical shapes.

SIMPLE MACHINES

Simple machines make it easier to do work. A wheel and axle make it easier to move objects across a surface by reducing friction. Pulleys, levers, inclined planes, screws, and wedges increase the force applied to an object. In this section, you will build a mail-delivery pulley and a simple lever.

UP-DOWN MAILBOX

Long before email and text messages, there was real mail! Build a pulley-powered mailbox that you can use to easily deliver mail from up high to down low.

WHAT YOU'LL NEED

- ☐ Hole punch
- ☐ Clean, empty yogurt cup
- ☐ Scissors
- ☐ String
- ☐ A high place that opens to a low place, like an open stairwell, a window, or a table
- ☐ Empty spool
- ☐ Painter's tape
- ☐ 2 bamboo skewers with the pointy tips cut off

1. Use the hole punch to punch 3 holes just under the rim of the yogurt cup. The holes should be an equal distance apart.

2. Use scissors to cut 3 lengths of string, each 1 foot long.

3. Use scissors to cut a length of string that reaches from the top of your high place to the bottom of your low place, plus 1 foot.

4. Thread a 1-foot piece of string through each of the holes in the cup.

STEPS 1 – 4

CONTINUED →

5. Gather the 6 ends of the short pieces of string and 1 end of the long piece of string.

6. Tie all 7 string ends in a single knot.

7. Tape the untied end of the long string to the empty spool with painter's tape. Wind the string onto the spool.

STEP 6

8. Tape the 2 bamboo skewers onto the top edge of a high place such as a windowsill or the top of a table as shown in the illustration on page 83. The skewers should be parallel and between 2 and 6 inches apart.

9. Run the string over 1 skewer. Place the spool on the other skewer so that the string winds under the skewer.

STEP 7

10. Try lifting and lowering materials by placing them in the cup and putting your pulley to work. Notice how the pulley makes it easy to lift whatever is in the cup!

STEP 10

⇒*FUN TIP*⇐ Try sending mail up and down with your homemade pulley system! Place a note inside the cup and lower it down. Ask a friend to read the note and reply, then wind the string around the spool to retrieve the message.

LIFTING LEVER

Would you believe you can lift 4 nickels with 1 nickel? You can—if you use a lever!

WHAT YOU'LL NEED

☐ Binder clip
☐ 12-inch ruler
☐ 5 nickels

1. Take the metal clips out of the binder clip by pinching the sides together and pulling them out of the tubes.

2. Set the binder clip, wide-side down, on a table. Balance the ruler on the clip so that the 6-inch mark is lined up over the clip.

STEP 2

3. Place 4 nickels in a stack on the 1-inch end of the ruler.

4. Place 1 nickel on the 12-inch end of the ruler.

5. Gently lift the ruler and shift the clip so that it is just under the 3-inch mark. The ruler should tip so that the heavier stack of nickels is lifted. Moving the fulcrum, or the point at which the lever balances, closer to a weight makes it much easier to lift the weight.

STEP 5

THE INVENTION OF THE WHEEL

The wheel, one of the most important simple machines in human history, was invented about 5,000 years ago, in Mesopotamia, an ancient civilization in the Middle East. Wheels were not complicated inventions, but they made a big impact. Wheels helped humans move heavy objects across land and were used in wheelbarrows, chariots, farming, pottery, and flour mills.

ADVENTURE GIRL CHALLENGE

Move a heavy book across a table using a simple wheel system. Set 10 pencils on the table. Place a book on top of the pencils. Push the book and watch it roll across the table! The pencils are like the logs that ancient people placed under heavy stones to move them across the land.

OCEAN LIFE

Oceans cover 70 percent of Earth and are often cold and dark—not great places for human life. Nevertheless, the oceans are full of living creatures that have made incredible adaptations to help them thrive in salt water. In this section, you will build a jellyfish toy, learn how fish float, and explore the properties of sand.

SQUISHY JELLYFISH TOY

Did you know that jellyfish don't have brains? Build a brainless fabric jellyfish filled with stuffing and tied with ribbon tentacles.

WHAT YOU'LL NEED

- ☐ 12-inch square of fleece
- ☐ 6-inch square of fleece
- ☐ Fabric scissors
- ☐ 8 ribbons, each 16 to 20 inches long
- ☐ Stuffing
- ☐ 2 googly eyes
- ☐ Fabric glue

1. Fold the 12-inch square of fleece into quarters and trim the folded edges into a quarter-circle shape. When you unfold the fleece, you will have a full circle.

2. Repeat step 1 with the 6-inch square of fleece to create a second, smaller circle.

3. Cut 8 small slits, ½ inch from the edge of the fabric, around both fabric circles. To cut each slit, pinch a small area of fabric and cut with scissors. Try to make the slits an equal distance apart.

STEPS 3 & 4

4. Lay the 6-inch circle on top of the 12-inch circle, lining up one of the openings in the smaller circle with an opening in the larger circle.

CONTINUED →

SQUISHY JELLYFISH TOY CONTINUED

5. Fold a ribbon in half and pass the fold through the aligned openings.

6. Pull the loose ends of the ribbon through the loop and tighten to make a tie, attaching the 2 circles.

7. Continue working around the circles until 7 of the 8 pairs of openings are tied with ribbon.

8. Fill the inside of the toy with stuffing to create the jellyfish's body.

9. Tie the last pair of openings together with the last ribbon.

10. Glue 2 googly eyes to your jellyfish using fabric glue.

STEP 5

STEP 6

STEP 7

STEP 8

FISH FLOAT

Fish can control where they float in the ocean using their swim bladder, an organ that fish can fill with different amounts of air. In this activity, you will use a glass bottle to represent a fish and adjust the amount of air inside the bottle to change where it floats.

WHAT YOU'LL NEED

☐ Sink
☐ Water
☐ Glass bottle with a cap or lid
☐ Food coloring

1. Fill the sink about 6 inches deep with water.

2. Fill the glass bottle with water. Add 1 drop of food coloring. Firmly screw on the bottle cap.

3. Place the bottle in the sink. It should rest at the bottom of the sink.

4. Remove the bottle and pour half of the water out so that the bottle is half full. Screw on the cap and place the bottle back in the sink. The bottle won't sink to the bottom, but it won't float on top of the water, either—it should hover somewhere in between. This is just like a fish swimming in the ocean!

STEP 2

CONTINUED →

5. Remove the bottle again and pour half of the remaining water out so that the bottle is one-quarter full. Screw on the cap and place the bottle back in the sink. It will float higher in the water and might even float on top of the water. Fish can change their depth in the ocean in the same way that you changed the depth of the bottle in the sink—by adjusting the amount of air inside.

STEP 5

≷FUN TIP≷ Use 2 plastic water bottles, one filled with water, the other filled with vegetable oil, to see which makes a better swim bladder.

ADVENTURE GIRL CHALLENGE

Visit your local library to find books on ocean life, including coral reefs, sea turtle migration, whale communication, mangroves, and bioluminescence. The ocean is full of wonders to explore!

KINETIC SAND

Sand has different properties at the bottom of the ocean, at the tide line, and high on the beach. In this craft, you will make kinetic sand, a fun, moldable toy that is a little bit wet without being sticky or slimy.

WHAT YOU'LL NEED

- ☐ 1 ¼ cups (1 pound) of sand, plain or colored
- ☐ Resealable plastic container
- ☐ ½ cup of cornstarch
- ☐ ¼ cup of vegetable oil
- ☐ Spoon

1. Measure 1 ¼ cups of sand into the resealable plastic container.

2. Add ½ cup of cornstarch to the sand and mix well with the spoon. Use the back of the spoon to break up any cornstarch lumps.

3. Add ¼ cup of vegetable oil to the container.

4. Stir the mixture with the spoon or your hands until there are no dry spots or oily spots.

5. Enjoy your kinetic sand! You can mold it into shapes, play with it, or use it as a calming fidget.

SYLVIA EARLE

(1935–)

is a marine biologist and a brilliant researcher of ocean life. She was a leader in developing the SCUBA and deep-sea submarine technology that allow scientists to dive deep into the ocean to study new creatures. Sylvia says, "You should treat the ocean as if your life depends on it, because it does."

OVER THE RAINBOW

Sunlight is made of all the colors of a rainbow. When sunlight bumps into water droplets, the colors in the light bounce, bend, and move apart. In this section, you will play with water and light to make a rainbow and build a spectroscope, a gadget used to measure the colors within sunlight.

SPECTACULAR SPECTROSCOPE

Scientists use complex spectroscopes—machines that divide light into different colors—to make exact measurements of specific colors. You can make a simple spectroscope with everyday items at home!

WHAT YOU'LL NEED

- X-Acto knife (optional)
- Scissors
- Paper towel tube
- 2 cardboard pieces, about 4 inches square, cut out of a cardboard box
- Pencil
- Painter's tape or masking tape
- CD

⚠ **CAUTION:** Have an adult do steps involving poking with scissors or using an X-Acto knife.

1. Have an adult use scissors or an X-Acto knife to create a U-shaped cut near one end of the paper towel tube.

2. Have an adult use scissors or an X-Acto knife to cut a rectangular opening in the paper tube, directly across from the U-shaped cut.

3. Place the tube vertically over a 4-inch cardboard square and trace it with a pencil.

STEP 1

STEP 2

CONTINUED →

4. Use scissors to cut around the circle you traced, leaving about ¼ inch of extra space around the circle.

5. Place the cardboard circle on top of the second cardboard square, which will serve as a safe cutting surface. Have an adult use scissors or an X-Acto knife to cut a rectangle out of the circle.

STEP 4

6. Place the cardboard circle on top of the tube at the other end from the U-shaped line. Use tape to attach the circle to the tube, avoiding the rectangular opening.

7. Slip the CD into the U-shaped cut, with the shiny side facing toward the tube.

8. Take your spectroscope outside. Hold it in a sunbeam so the light shines in through the side of the tube and onto the CD.

STEP 6

9. Look into the spectroscope through the rectangular opening at the top of the tube. Rotate your spectroscope to catch the light on the CD until you see a rainbow shining on the inside walls of the tube.

RAINBOW IN A BOWL

Use a mirror to amplify the rainbow-making power of water in this quick and fun activity!

WHAT YOU'LL NEED

- ☐ Bowl half full of water
- ☐ Sunbeam
- ☐ Small mirror

1. Fill a bowl halfway with water.

2. Place the bowl of water near a sunny window.

3. Place the mirror in the bowl so that it catches the light.

4. With your eyes on the ceiling, tilt the mirror until it catches a sunbeam. The mirror will shoot a rainbow onto the ceiling.

STEP 4

CONTINUED →

12 TYPES OF RAINBOWS

Scientists have officially named 12 types of rainbows, including the common single bow shape as well as full circles, double bows, and twinned bows. Rainbows can be made by rain, fog, sleet, or sea spray in sunlight or moonlight.

⇒*FUN TIP*⇐ Try holding a white piece of paper over your rainbow bowl. Can you catch a rainbow on the paper?

ADVENTURE GIRL CHALLENGE

Fill your room with rainbows! Place a prism in a window, wait for a sunny moment, then shift the prism to throw rainbows around the room.

ALL ABOUT GRAVITY

Gravity is a force that pulls objects in the universe together. Bigger objects have stronger gravity. Because we are very close to a very big object (Earth!), the only gravity we really notice is Earth's. In this section, you will play with gravity's effects using a ball-bounce game and a half-pipe racetrack.

BOUNCE GAME BOX

Gravity always pulls objects down to Earth's surface at the same speed. With practice, you can use gravity to make a ball bounce into an exact spot—like in this cool ball-bounce game box.

WHAT YOU'LL NEED

- ☐ Scissors
- ☐ Shoebox, or a cardboard box about the same size
- ☐ Marker
- ☐ Pushpin or pen
- ☐ 6 chopsticks
- ☐ Ping-Pong ball
- ☐ Painter's tape

1. Remove the lid from the box. If the box has flaps instead of a lid, use scissors to cut the flaps off.

2. Use a marker to draw 6 equally spaced dots on the bottom of the box.

3. Use a pushpin or pen to make a small hole at each dot.

4. Press a chopstick into each hole.

5. Place your game box on the floor against a wall.

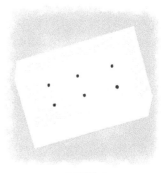

STEP 2

STEP 4

CONTINUED →

6. Stand about 3 feet away from the game box with a Ping-Pong ball in your hand. Place a piece of painter's tape at your feet to mark your spot so that you always throw from the same place.

7. Throw the ball on the floor and watch how it bounces up.

8. Keep throwing the ball until you can make it bounce and then land in the box between the chopsticks.

STEP 6

⋛*FUN TIP*⋚ For a more challenging ball-bounce game box, use more chopsticks and place them closer together. To make the game easier, use fewer chopsticks and place them farther apart.

HALF-PIPE RACETRACK

In extreme, gravity-defying sports like snowboarding and freestyle BMX, a half-pipe is a half tube used to perform daring tricks. In this activity, you will build a half-pipe track and watch a Ping-Pong ball experience extreme gravity.

WHAT YOU'LL NEED

- ☐ Scissors
- ☐ 5 cardboard tubes, such as paper towel tubes
- ☐ Painter's tape
- ☐ Wall
- ☐ Ping-Pong ball, bouncy ball, or racecar

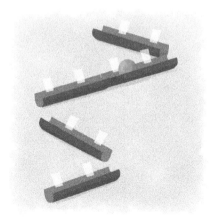

1. Use scissors to cut the 5 cardboard tubes in half lengthwise. When you are finished, you should have 10 long half tubes.

2. Use painter's tape to attach one half tube to a wall at your eye level, angling the half tube so that one end is higher than the other.

3. Continue taping all your half tubes to the wall to make a track. You can make a zigzag pattern or a straight diagonal line, but just make sure that one end of each tube is always higher than the other. Also make sure that the second tube is lower than the first tube, the third tube is lower than the second tube, and so on, so the path goes continually downward.

4. Once your track is completed, place a Ping-Pong ball at the top of your half-pipe track. Let it go.

CONTINUED →

5. What happened? Did the Ping-Pong ball go flying off the track? Did it fall between the half tubes? Use more painter's tape to adjust your half-pipe track and do another run.

6. Keep playing and changing your half-pipe track to get your Ping-Pong ball to do some gnarly tricks—like dropping a foot from one half tube to the next or flying across the room before it lands!

LUNAR GRAVITY

The Moon is much smaller than Earth, but it is still pretty big and has a strong gravitational pull. The ocean water on the side of Earth that's closest to the Moon gets pulled so strongly by lunar gravity that the ocean actually bulges out and away from Earth! Ocean water rises and falls regularly because the bulge changes as Earth spins on its axis.

CODER CLUB

Coding involves translating instructions into a language that a computer can understand. Whenever a person develops an app, website, or software program, they give very precise instructions in one of many coding languages. In this section, you'll learn to use a binary (two-part) coding language by making jewelry, and you'll practice delivering precise instructions by setting up a treasure hunt!

BINARY JEWELRY

Binary code, which uses just 2 symbols, is one of the most basic computer languages. In this craft, you'll use 2 colors of beads to code a binary message into a necklace.

WHAT YOU'LL NEED

☐ Black beads
☐ White beads
☐ Beading cord,
   2 to 3 feet long

1. Get ready to code your name into a necklace! Each letter will be 8 beads long once you code it. For example, if you code a 5-letter name, your necklace will be 40 beads long. A 10-letter name will be 80 beads long.

2. Look at the chart (below) of the official binary code for the capital letter alphabet. Find the first letter of your name.

3. For a 0, put a white bead on your string. For a 1, add a black bead. For example, coding the letter *R* on your string would create the following bead pattern: white, black, white, black, white, white, black, white.

BINARY

A	01000001	N	01001110
B	01000010	O	01001111
C	01000011	P	01010000
D	01000100	Q	01010001
E	01000101	R	01010010
F	01000110	S	01010011
G	01000111	T	01010100
H	01001000	U	01010101
I	01001001	V	01010110
J	01001010	W	01010111
K	01001011	X	01011000
L	01001100	Y	01011001
M	01001101	Z	01011010

CONTINUED →

4. Continue beading until you have included all the letters in your name.

5. Bring both ends of the beading cord together. Tie them together in a single knot by making a loop and passing the ends through the loop. Can you figure out what name is spelled in the illustration?

> ⇒*FUN TIP*⇐ Try beading a coded necklace with beads of 2 colors instead of black and white.

ADVENTURE GIRL CHALLENGE

Make a necklace for a friend with a secret message coded into the beads. Be sure to include the binary alphabet chart so they can decode your gift!

CODER SAYS!

Providing clear, specific directions is essential in coding. In this activity, you'll practice this skill by writing directions for a friend to find a hidden treasure.

WHAT YOU'LL NEED

- [ ] A fun object to hide, like a toy, gadget, or book
- [ ] A place to hide the object
- [ ] Pencil
- [ ] Paper

1. Hide the object in your home or yard.

2. Choose a starting point for your treasure hunt.

3. Slowly travel from your starting point to your hiding place, noticing how many steps and turns you take. Your path needs to be made of straight lines and left or right turns, with no curves.

4. Go back to the starting point.

5. Use a pencil and paper to write clear, specific directions for every step needed to travel from the starting point to the hiding place.

6. Give your directions to a friend or family member. Lead them to the starting place and have them follow your written directions. Don't say anything! Let your directions be their only guide.

7. Were they able to find the hidden object? If you gave advice to another coder about writing great directions, what would you say?

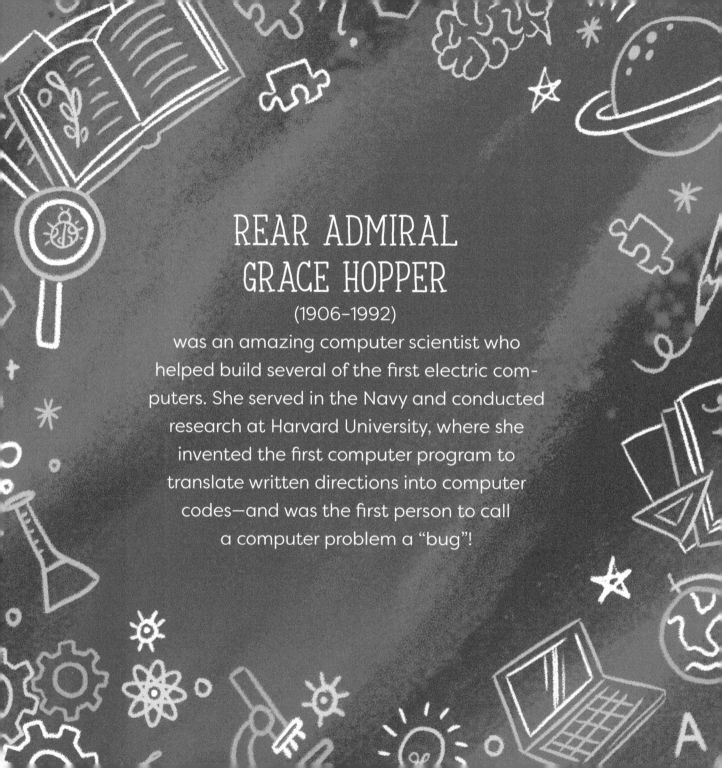

REAR ADMIRAL GRACE HOPPER

(1906–1992)

was an amazing computer scientist who helped build several of the first electric computers. She served in the Navy and conducted research at Harvard University, where she invented the first computer program to translate written directions into computer codes—and was the first person to call a computer problem a "bug"!

THE ABCS OF DNA

DNA is an incredibly special chemical. Made of 4 building blocks, DNA holds the code to life: Living things use the instructions in DNA to grow and develop. In this section, you will craft a chain similar to DNA and practice DNA coding. What is in an Adventure Girl's DNA? The desire to learn and explore, of course!

KNITTED DNA GARLAND

DNA's shape is like a twisted ladder. Two-finger knitting can create a double chain that is like DNA's and makes a great decoration!

WHAT YOU'LL NEED

- ☐ Yarn (about ⅓ skein)
- ☐ Scissors
- ☐ Pom-poms in 4 colors
- ☐ Glue

STEPS 1 – 5

1. Place the end of a ball of yarn in the palm of your nondominant hand (the hand you use less often).

2. Hold the yarn 5 inches from the end with your thumb. With your palm facing you, bring the yarn behind your pointer finger at the base of your finger.

3. Bring the yarn in front of your middle finger. Wrap the yarn around your finger so that it goes behind your middle finger. Then wrap it over the front of your pointer finger.

4. Bring the yarn behind your pointer finger and repeat step 3. You should now have 2 loops woven around each of your 2 fingers. Let the long end of yarn fall behind your hand.

5. Gently tug the lower loop on your pointer finger over the upper loop and off your finger. Repeat with the lower loop on your middle finger.

CONTINUED →

6. You will have one loop left on each finger. Push these loops down to the base of your fingers.

7. Repeat steps 3 to 6 until your garland is as long as you'd like it to be.

8. With scissors, cut the long end of yarn about 12 inches from your hand. Bring the tail through the loop on your middle finger, back to front, then through the loop on your pointer finger, front to back. Pull tight.

STEP 6

9. Organize your 4 colors of pom-poms in pairs, with the same 2 colors always paired together. Glue the pom-pom pairs on opposite sides of your garland to represent the DNA code.

10. Hang your garland over your bed or in a window to make a DNA decoration!

STEP 7

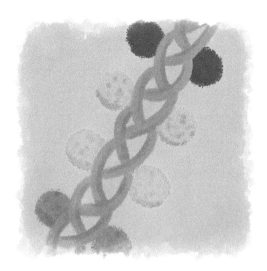

ADVENTURE GIRL CHALLENGE

Make a DNA bracelet by threading pony bead color pairs (like your pom-pom color pairs) onto 2 pipe cleaners, then twisting the ends together.

LIFE'S CODED MESSAGE

The DNA code describes the building blocks of living things using a 3-letter code. DNA is spelled out in letters. Every 3 letters make a codon that tells a living cell how to make matching RNA. The matching RNA has 3 different letters that make an anticodon that tells the cell how to pick out an amino acid, the building block of a protein. The billions of letters in DNA translate to the proteins that make up living things—3 letters at a time! In this activity, you will invent a 3-color code to trade messages with a friend.

WHAT YOU'LL NEED

- ☐ Paper
- ☐ Markers, in at least 4 colors
- ☐ Envelope

1. On a sheet of paper, set up a decoding chart, with "color code" on the left side of the paper and "word" on the right side.

2. Draw 3 dots of different colors on the "color code" side.

3. Pick a word that you would like to use in your messages and write it across from the 3 dots on the "word" side.

4. Keep making new 3-dot patterns and matching them with words for your messages until you have at least 10 words.

5. Decide what message you would like to write with the words you coded.

6. On another sheet of paper, draw the dots that represent the words of your message.

7. Make a copy of your decoding chart.

8. Place your message, the decoding chart, and a blank sheet of paper in an envelope.

9. Give the envelope to a friend. Invite them to write a response to your message using the blank sheet of paper.

10. Enjoy sharing messages using your secret code!

DNA-MATCHING GENES

Most living things have very similar DNA codes. Would you believe 99.9 percent of the DNA codes in all humans match? Human DNA codes match 80 to 99 percent of the codes in other mammals, including cats, cows, and chimpanzees. You even have 60 percent of the same DNA codes as a banana! This means that the 40 percent that are different code some really important stuff. It also means that if someone says, "You're bananas," they are 60 percent right!

10 WOMEN IN STEM THROUGH HISTORY

 **Augusta Ada King, Countess of Lovelace** (1815–1852), was an English noblewoman who hosted famous mathematicians in her home. Ada Lovelace is considered to be the first computer programmer.

 **Marie Curie, Chemist** (1867–1934), the first woman to win a Nobel prize, was a chemist and physicist. She discovered radioactivity and helped develop X-ray technologies.

 **Edith Clarke, Electrical Engineer** (1883–1959), invented an early graphing calculator, helped design dams that make electricity, and wrote an electrical engineering textbook.

 **Barbara McClintock, Geneticist** (1902–1992), began her career as a plant scientist. Her studies of corn DNA led her to the discovery that genes can move and change activity levels.

 **Rachel Carson, Environmental Scientist** (1907–1964), while working in marine biology, noticed how pesticides hurt living things. Her writing changed how people thought about pollution and sparked the American environmentalist movement.

Dorothy Vaughan, Mathematician (1910–2008), began working for NASA during World War II. She did complex math and computer programming work that made early space missions possible. You can learn more about Dorothy Vaughan and other "human computers" in the movie *Hidden Figures*.

Chien-Shiung Wu, Physicist (1912–1997), moved to the United States from China to study physics. She studied atoms and their parts, helping to develop nuclear power and to understand disease.

Rosalind Franklin, Molecular Biologist (1920–1958), was an English scientist who is most famous for taking the first photos of DNA. Her research also photos of DNA. Her research also led to important discoveries about viruses, RNA, and coal.

Susan Kare, Iconographer (1954–), is an American designer of computer interfaces. Her work has contributed to the way people see and use products from Apple, Microsoft, IBM, Sony, Facebook, and Pinterest.

Adriana Ocampo, Planetary Geologist (1955–), is a Colombian earth scientist who helped discover the crater from the asteroid impact that killed the dinosaurs. She has worked on NASA space missions to several planets.

ACKNOWLEDGMENTS

Thanks to my computer science teacher colleagues at Open World Learning Community for helping me learn about women programmers, to Greg Leifeld for teaching me about trusses and joists, to Dylan Bickelhall for introducing me to hexaflexagons, to Rosalea Bickelhall for teaching me how to finger knit, and to the Callisto team for putting together a fun and beautiful book.

ABOUT THE AUTHOR

Megan Olivia Hall, PHD, MAED is the 2013 Minnesota Teacher of the Year. As a science teacher, Megan has worked with learners of many ages and levels, from kindergarteners to graduate students. A National Board Certified teacher, she teaches science and agriculture at Open World Learning Community in St. Paul Public Schools. Her books include *Awesome Kitchen Science Experiments for Kids*, *Awesome Outdoor Science Experiments for Kids*, and *Big Chemistry Experiments for Little Kids*. A Leading Educator Ambassador for Equity fellow with the Education Civil Rights Alliance, Megan holds a PhD in learning, instruction, and innovation from Walden University.

ABOUT THE ILLUSTRATOR

Cait Brennan is an easily excited illustrator. Her work celebrates peaceful moments in nature, kids and kids at heart, travel, and adventures of all sizes. She works on a variety of projects but has a particular passion for illustrating books. Her favorite projects are ones that transport you into another world where your imagination roams free. In addition to drawing a lot, Cait loves making big messes in the kitchen and exploring dusty antique shops.